134

THE BEAUTY OF STEAM

Written By
Peter Waller

Danann
BOOKS

Danann
BOOKAZINES

© Danann Publishing Ltd

CONTENTS

INTRODUCTION 4

EASTERN/NORTH EASTERN REGIONS 6

LONDON MIDLAND REGION 26

SCOTTISH REGION 44

SOUTHERN REGION 64

WESTERN REGION 84

INTRODUCTION

When British Railways was established in 1948, it inherited some 28,000 steam locomotives. Over the next decade, until production ceased, several thousand new locomotives were added, primarily to replace older and less powerful types. Initially, many of the new locomotives built were constructed to designs produced by the 'Big Four' railway companies but the bulk of the new locomotives comprised large numbers of ex-War Department 'Austerity' 2-8-0 and 2-10-0 freight locomotives and the 999 BR Standard types. However, despite all this investment, less than a generation after Nationalisation main-line steam in Britain came to an end. Steam was to survive, courtesy of the numerous preservation societies that took on closed lines from the 1950s onwards, but an essential part of the British landscape for almost 150 years had been consigned to history as far as British Railways was concerned.

There had been some early experimentation in diesel and electric traction before Nationalisation; the London, Midland & Scottish had, for example, introduced the first two main-line diesel-electrics and the London & North Eastern was developing the first electrified main line – the Woodhead route across the Pennines, a project completed by BR in the early 1950s – but steam reigned supreme over the bulk of the railway network, inspiring a generation of railway enthusiasts. Steam seemed to have all the advantages as, primarily, it relied on home-produced fuel – coal – rather than the imported oil required for diesel operation; the latter cost foreign exchange – money that the country did not have as it faced post-war austerity and the need to rebuild after World War 2.

The first real threat to the dominance of steam came with the Modernisation Plan of 1955; this foreshadowed the replacement of steam over several decades, with its replacement by main-line electrification and by the widespread adoption of diesel traction. The first new diesel multiple-units, which had been introduced prior to the Plan, had demonstrated that cleaner and faster trains could draw passengers back to the railways, essential at a time when the rise in private car ownership was significant and leading to a loss of passenger traffic on many lines. The Plan envisaged significant investment in the railway industry but, and this was the major drawback to the scheme, this was to be funded by borrowing.

Over the next few years, as the railway's finances continued to deteriorate, the interest charges on the borrowed funds added considerably to the losses that the railway industry was facing. At the time there was no concept of the 'social railway' – lines subsidised for the benefit of the communities they served – and British Railways (along with the overall British Transport Commission) was expected to be profitable. It was against this background that the then Minister of Transport, Ernest Marples, brought in an outsider – Dr Richard Beeching from the giant ICI – to take over as chairman of British Railways. Beeching was tasked with trying to make the railways profitable and, in furtherance of this, he undertook the research into a major report on the industry's future. When published in March 1963, Beeching's report – The Reshaping of British Railways – was a bombshell; it recommended the closure of a significant proportion of the surviving passenger network – although it should be stressed that closures had been an ongoing process from the late 1920s onwards – as well as a retreat from several types of traditional traffic. Not all was negative, Beeching saw a future in certain types of freight and advocated investment in its development.

The consequence was that the existing programme of closures was accelerated. Passenger lines the length and breadth of the realm disappeared as did many of those lines that had survived for freight traffic only. With the closures came the realisation that BR had vastly more locomotives – diesel as well as steam – than were required for the ongoing business with the result that the elimination of main-line steam was achieved much more rapidly than the planners of the 1950s might have conceived. Thus locomotives that might have expected to be in service into the 1980s were withdrawn and scrapped with less than a decade of operation. The summer of 1968 witnessed the final timetabled main-line steam operation and, on 11 August 1968 with the operation of the 'Fifteen Guinea' special, a way of life came to an end.

Of course, it was not really the end; the allure of steam remained. Preservation meant that it was still possible to experience steam and, courtesy of the famous Woodham Bros scrapyard in South Wales, numerous locomotives were resurrected from their supposedly final resting place. Even British Railways saw main-line steam return when, in October 1971, 'King' class No 6000 King George V hauled the first 'Return to Steam' special. Almost 50 years on from that event main-line and preservation steam ensure that current and future generations can enjoy the beauty of steam.

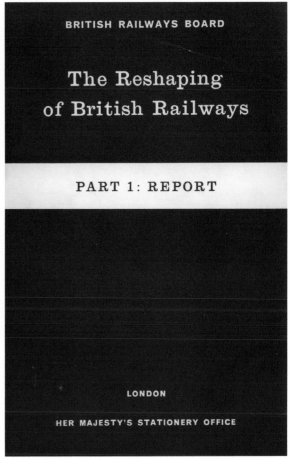

ABOVE LEFT

The Eastern Region timetable for the period from September 1960 to June 1961. Each of the six BR regions had a separate corporate colour; for the Eastern Region it was dark blue. *Author's Collection*

ABOVE MIDDLE

The Western Region's corporate colour was dark brown; this is shown to good effect on the region's timetable for September 1961 to June 1962. By this date diesel-hydraulic locomotives were increasingly replacing steam on the main line from London Paddington to Bristol, South Wales and the West Country. *Author's Collection.*

ABOVE RIGHT

The front cover of The Reshaping of British Railways; appearing in March 1963 the report represented a radical attempt to restore the railway's finances at a time when the concept of the 'social railway' did not exist. Although its author, Dr Richard Beeching, was heavily criticised at the time and subsequently, it was the politicians who ultimately took the decision as to which lines closed and which survived. *Author's Collection*

A NOTE ON THE PHOTOGRAPHS

All of the photographs reproduced in this book have been drawn from the collection of the Online Transport Archive, a UK-registered charity that was set up to accommodate collections put together by transport enthusiasts who wished to see their precious images secured for the long-term. Further information about the archive can be found at: www.onlinetransportarchive.org or email secretary@onlinetransportarchive.org

EASTERN/NORTH EASTERN REGIONS

These two regions were formed out of the LNER's operations in England. The Eastern Region was effectively the lines inherited by the LNER from the Great Central, Great Eastern and Great Northern railways and stretched from East Anglia and London to York, the West Riding of Yorkshire and, courtesy of the GC's ownership of the Wrexham, Mold & Connah's Quay Railway, to Cheshire and the Welsh Marches. The North Eastern was effectively a recreation of the erstwhile North Eastern Railway, which had already absorbed the smaller Hull & Barnsley before the Grouping in 1923, and covered the North and East Ridings of Yorkshire, County Durham and Northumberland. The region also extended into the north-west of England courtesy of the transpennine route via Stainmore. The Eastern corporate colour was dark blue whilst the North Eastern's was orange. The Eastern Region's remit was amongst the first to be altered as it assumed control of the ex-LMS London, Tilbury & Southend Railway routes in 1949. More significant change came during the 1950s with, for example, the transfer of the Great Central main line to the LMR. With the reduction in railway mileage during the 1960s, the two regions were combined into a single Eastern Region in 1967.

MAIN IMAGE

Pictured passing through Retford station non-stop with an Up service heading south towards King's Cross is Gresley-designed Class V2 2-6-2 No 60890. This was one of 184 of this versatile type of mixed traffic locomotive constructed for the LNER between 1936 and 1944. No 60890 was completed at Darlington Works in December 1939. Although the class was still intact at the end of 1961, withdrawals — including No 60890 — commenced the following year and 69 had been withdrawn by the end of 1962. The last were to be taken out of service in 1966. *John McCann/Online Transport Archive*

Pictured passing through Potters Bar station with an up service towards King's Cross in early 1952 is 'A1' Pacific No 60131 Osprey. At this date the locomotive was still relatively new, having been built at Darlington Works in October 1948. Originally painted in LNER green, No 60131 emerged in BR blue in June 1950, when it was also officially named, but was to be repainted again, this time into Brunswick Green, in September 1951 when it was reallocated to Grantham shed. Surviving until October 1965, No 60131 had one of the longest careers of any locomotive in the class. *John McCann/Online Transport Archive*

Although designed originally by Ivatt for the LMS, only three of this class of 2-6-0 were completed prior to Nationalisation with a further 159 being completed by BR before production ceased in September 1952. Peterborough (Spital)-allocated No 43068 — seen here on 2 June 1951 at Bourne with a service towards Essendine — was one of those built at Doncaster and was completed in December 1950 and so was virtually brand new when recorded here. By this date the branch from Essendine, on the East Coast main line, to Bourne was in its last month; passenger services were withdrawn on 18 June. *Peter N. Williams/Online Transport Archive*

Pictured at North Woolwich at the head of a Railway Correspondence & Travel Society special on 8 April 1951 is Class J69 0-6-0 No E8619. The locomotive has yet to be renumbered by BR — it was not to be so treated until June 1953, the last of the class to be dealt with — with the 'E' signifying that it was a locomotive inherited from the LNER. The 'J67' and 'J69' classes, visually very similar, were both designed by Holden for the GER; the former primarily for freight traffic and the latter for use on suburban passenger services out of Liverpool Street. A total of 160 of the two types were completed, of which 134 passed to BR in 1948. No 68619, as the locomotive became, was completed at Stratford Works in May 1904. Sister locomotive No 68633 survives in preservation. *Peter N. Williams/Online Transport Archive*

Following Nationalisation, the new BR continued to build new steam locomotives based around the designs it inherited. In 1951, however, the first of 999 Standard locomotives, designed by Robert A. Riddles, emerged; this was 'Britannia' class Pacific No 70000 Britannia, which is seen here in service on the Eastern Region when virtually brand new. The inspiration for the name came from noted railway photographer — and future Bishop of Wakefield — Eric Treacy and in all 55 members of the class were constructed at Crewe between 1951 and 1954 with many providing sterling service on the main lines of East Anglia. Although initially considered for preservation, No 70000 was in poor mechanical condition and so No 70013 Oliver Cromwell was selected to form part of the National Collection but No 70000 was to survive as well, being purchased privately Britannia Locomotive Society. *D. Kelk/Online Transport Archive*

The Chesham branch, which extends for almost four miles from the junction at Chalfont, was opened by the Metropolitan Railway in 1889. Although the Metropolitan was to become part of the London Passenger Transport Board network in July 1933, operation of the remaining steam-hauled services north of Rickmansworth towards Aylesbury and the branch to Chesham was passed to the LNER. This continued until the line south of Chalfont and the Chesham branch were electrified for use by London Underground stock in 1960. On Sunday 27 March 1954 ex-LNER Class C13 4-4-2T No 67418, one of a class of 40 built by the Great Central between 1903 and 1905, stands at Chesham with a service to Chalfont. *Neil Davenport/Online Transport Archive*

Until the completion of the Humber Bridge in 1981, there was a railway-owned ferry service linking New Holland Pier with central Hull. On 3 August 1951 Class N5 0-6-2T No 69322 stands at the railway station that served the pier awaiting departure with a service towards Grimsby and Cleethorpes. The first three of the class were completed during 1891 and 1892 at the Gorton Works of the Manchester, Sheffield & Lincolnshire Railway — predecessor of the Great Central — to a design of Parker. The locomotives were the first in Britain to be fitted with the Belpaire firebox. A further 124 were built between 1893 and 1901. The locomotives were slightly modified by Gresley, with stovepipe chimneys — as seen on No 69322 — replacing the original. At Nationalisation 121 of the class passed to BR but all had been withdrawn by the end of 1959; No 69322 succumbed in August of that year. None survive in preservation. *Peter N. Williams/Online Transport Archive*

Seen departing from Sheffield Victoria in May 1952 with an eastbound service is Thompson 'B1' class 4-6-0 No 61305; this was one of the class that was built by North British and was completed in April 1948. At this stage Victoria station was still without the 1,500V dc overhead electrification; work was in progress at this time on the completion of the Woodhead electrification plan and electric passenger services from Victoria west towards Penistone and Manchester would be introduced in September 1954. *John McCann/Online Transport Archive*

On 20 June 1954 two ex-LNER 0-6-0s stand at Selby station. On the left is ex-NER Class J21 No 65078 and on the right is ex-GCR Class J11 No 64419. The latter had brought the Railway Correspondence & Travel Society 'South Yorkshire Rail Tour No 3' on a circuitous route from Sheffield Midland to Selby whilst No 65078 was to take the train on towards Barlby and then to York via the Derwent Valley Light Railway. Worsdell-designed No 65078 was built at Darlington in April 1891 and was one of 83 of the once 201-strong class to pass to BR in 1948; it was withdrawn in March 1957. One of the class — No 65033 — survives in preservation. No 64419 was one of 174 locomotives built to Robinson's design for the Great Central between September 1901 and May 1910; completed at Gorton Works in August 1907, No 64419 was to achieve exactly 55 years of service when withdrawn in August 1962. None of the 'J11s' were to be preserved. *John McCann/Online Transport Archive*

On 18 September 1954 ex-LNER Class A3 No 60111 Enterprise heads southbound through Rugby Central station with an up service towards London Marylebone. No 60111 had originally been completed at Doncaster Works in August 1923 and was rebuilt as an 'A3' in July 1927. Four years after the date of this photograph, No 60111 was further rebuilt, this time gaining a double chimney. The section of the Great Central main line south from Rugby to Aylesbury lost its passenger services on 5 September 1966; those north to Nottingham, however, survived (operated by diesel multiple-units), until withdrawn on 5 May 1969. *John McCann/Online Transport Archive*

Standard 2-6-0 No 78019 was built at Darlington in March 1954 and was thus virtually brand new when recorded at Barras, on the ex-North Eastern Railway line from Barnard Castle to Kirkby Stephen via Stainmore, on 3 September 1954. In all 65 of this type of locomotive were constructed between December 1952 and November 1956 primarily for light passenger work. Although four members of the class — including No 78019 — survive in preservation, one of the quartet — No 78059 — is being restored as a 2-6-2T (No 84030) to recreate one of the Standard designs of which no example was originally preserved. *Neil Davenport/Online Transport Archive*

On 24 July 1955 the Railway Correspondence & Travel Society ran the 'Fensman' special from Liverpool Street to Cambridge behind 'Britannia' Pacific No 70037 *Hereward the Wake*; from Cambridge Class J17 No 65562 was employed to take the excursion over a number of lines to the north of the city. These included the branches to Mildenhall and Stoke Ferry. Here, the locomotive is seen being watered at St Ives prior to heading towards Ramsey East. A total of 90 'J17s' were constructed by the GER between 1900 and 1910; all bar one — the exception had been destroyed by enemy action in World War 2 — survived to pass to BR in 1948. The last were withdrawn in 1962 — No 65562 having succumbed in August 1958 — with one, No 65567, surviving into preservation. *John McCann/Online Transport Archive*

Courtesy of the Great Central Railway, the LNER inherited a number of lines in North Wales and Cheshire. The southernmost point served by ex-LNER services in the area was Wrexham Central where Class N5 0-6-2T No 63940 is pictured. In all BR inherited 121 'N5s' from the LNER; these had all been built for the GCR between 1891 and 1901. No 63940 was constructed at Gorton Works in June 1900 and was to see more than 50 years' service before withdrawal in June 1956. The last of the type were withdrawn by the end of 1960. *R. W. A. Jones/Online Transport Archive*

MAIN IMAGE

One of the earlier inter-regional transfers saw the ex-Midland London, Tilbury & Southend Railway route from Fenchurch Street to Shoeburyness transferred from the London Midland to the Eastern. To mark the centenary of the line in 1956 one of the LT&SR's 4-4-2Ts, No 41966, was restored as LT&SR No 80 *Thundersley* and the newly restored locomotive is recorded here on 11 March 1956 on the occasion of the Railway Correspondence & Travel Society 'Southend Centenary' special. No 80 was to be preserved following withdrawal in June 1956 and is now on static display at Bressingham. *John McCann/Online Transport Archive*

TOP

The final development of the great LNER Pacific type was 'A1' class; following the rebuilding by Thompson as modified by Peppercorn of No 60113 prior to Nationalisation, a further 49 Pacifics were constructed to Peppercorn's design between August 1948 and December 1949. No 60142 *Edward Fletcher*, seen here on a down freight at Heaton on 20 July 1957, was completed at Darlington in February 1949. Withdrawn in June 1965 , No 60142 was — like the remainder of the class — scrapped. More recently, however, the 50th of the type — No 60163 *Tornado* — has been built, the first main-line steam locomotive constructed in Britain since 1960. *Tony Wickens/ Online Transport Archive*

MIDDLE

Ulleskelf — an intermediate station on the ex-North Eastern line from Church Fenton to York — is the location of this view of Class D49 4-4-0 No 62731 Selkirkshire with a northbound service. Between 1927 and 1935 76 Class D49 4-4-0s were constructed at Darlington Works to the design of Nigel Gresley primarily for use on intermediate express passenger services on the LNER's ex-North British and North Eastern lines; the first 36 — later BR 62700-35 — were the 'Shire' class and designated Class 49/1. All 36 were withdrawn by mid-1961, with No 62731 succumbing in April 1959. *Paul de Beer/Online Transport Archive*

BOTTOM

Pictured at Marylebone station with the 10am service to Manchester is 'B1' class 4-6-0 No 61077 on 7 June 1958. Control of the ex-Great Central main line was transferred from the Eastern to London Midland Region during 1958; whilst there was no immediate change, the LMR regarded the route as duplicating the ex-Midland main line and, from 1960, a gradual run-down of the GC route commenced. Thompson designed the mixed traffic 'B1' as a replacement for a number of locomotives that the LNER had inherited. Introduced in 1942, wartime restrictions meant that construction was slow, with only 10 being completed by 1944. With peace restored, construction work resumed in 1946 and a further 400 were built between then and 1952. No 61077 was built by North British and new in September 1946. Two of the type were eventually preserved: No 61264, after a period at Woodham Bros's scrapyard (the only ex-LNER locomotive to end up there) and 61306. *Peter N. Williams/Online Transport Archive*

MAIN IMAGE

On 6 June 1959 Gresley Class A4 No 60015 *Quicksilver* heads the up 'Flying Scotsman' at St Neots heading towards London King's Cross. The second of the classic streamlined locomotives to be completed — at Doncaster Works in September 1935 — No 60015 had originally been LNER No 2510 when new. Unlike a number of other members of the class that saw a brief Indian Summer of service in Scotland when steam-hauled main-line services over the East Coast main line ceased, No 60015 was a relatively early casualty, being withdrawn in April 1963. *Paul de Beer/Online Transport Archive*

TOP

As the locomotive crew look out, one of the ex-GER Class J15 0-6-0s, No 65469, awaits departure from Wymondham towards Dereham with a freight. In all 289 of the Worsdell-designed locomotives were built between 1883 and 1913 of which 127 survived to be taken over the BR in January 1948. A familiar sight throughout the erstwhile GER system, the locomotives were employed on both passenger and freight turns. No 65469 was to be withdrawn in August 1962; sister No 65462 survives in preservation. R*oy Hobbs/Online Transport Archive*

MIDDLE

Although a total of 71 of the 'B12' class 4-6-0s had originally been built to a design of Holden for the Great Eastern Railway between 1911 and 1921 with a further 10 to a slightly modified design following in 1928, all bar one had been withdrawn by the end of 1959. The survivor — No 61572 seen here on Norwich shed in July 1961 — was one of the 10 constructed by Beyer Peacock in 1928. Like many of the class, No 61572 was one of those to be rebuilt to a Gresley design between 1932 and 1944. Withdrawn in September 1961, No 61572 was to be preserved and is now based on the North Norfolk Railway. *Roy Hobbs/Online Transport Archive*

BOTTOM

By 1962, steam on the metals of the erstwhile Great Eastern Railway was drawing to a close and, on 31 March of that year, the Railway Correspondence & Travel Society organised the 'Great Eastern Commemorative' rail tour. This started from Liverpool Street behind 'Britannia' class No 70003 John Bunyan before touring a number of lines in the Norwich area. The 'Britannia' picked up the train for the return journey via Ely and Cambridge at Thetford and the train is pictured there shortly before departure with the locomotive looking in pristine condition. The following year would see No 70003 transferred to London Midland Region, where it was allocated to Carlisle (Kingmoor) shed until final withdrawal. *Roy Hobbs/Online Transport Archive*

MAIN IMAGE

One of the Thompson-designed Class B1 4-6-0s — No 61283
— is pictured departing from Liverpool Street station in June
1962. *Roy Hobbs/Online Transport Archive*

ABOVE

Designed by Edward Thompson, Gresley's successor as the
LNER's CME, the 'L1' class 2-6-4T eventually numbered 100
locomotives constructed between 1945 and 1950. Designed
primarily for suburban services to London King's Cross and
Marylebone, one of the class — No 67735 — is pictured
departing from West Green with a service to Palace Gates.
Relatively few lines in Greater London were scheduled for
closure by Beeching; one of these was the ex-GER line to
Palace Gates. Passenger services were withdrawn on 7
January 1963. *Roy Hobbs/Online Transport Archive*

Evidence of the new order at Liverpool Street in June 1962 as,
on the left, one of the then-new Brush-built Type 2 diesel-
electric locomotives stands under the overhead installed for the
suburban electrification. Initially this had been 1,500V dc but, by
this date, had been converted to 6.25kV. On the right is Class
N7 0-6-2T No 69725. Designed for the GER by Hill, the first two
of the type were delivered in 1914, but it was not until 1921
that construction of the class continued. Designed for suburban
services out of Liverpool Street, in all 134 of the design were
built by 1928. Although all remained in service at the end of
1956, the electrification of the suburban services saw their rapid
elimination in the late 1950s and, by the end of 1961, only nine
— including No 69725 — remained in service. All had been
withdrawn by the end of the following year with No 69621 being
eventually preserved. *Roy Hobbs/ Online Transport Archive*

On 28 July 1962 Gresley Class A3 Pacific No 60088 *Book
Law* awaits departure from Newcastle Central. No 60088 was
a locally — Heaton — based locomotive when recorded here.
By this date, the 'A3' class had been modified by the fitting of
double chimneys and the majority had also been fitted with
smoke deflectors. No 60088 received the former in July 1959
and the latter in June 1961. One final reallocation saw No
60088 transferred to Gateshead, from where the locomotive
was withdrawn in October 1963. *Tony Wickens/Online
Transport Archive*

MAIN IMAGE

It's 9 March 1963 and steam operation on the southern end of the East Coast main line is drawing slowly to a close as Class A1 Pacific No 60120 *Kittiwake* heads northbound with a down evening parcels train. Completed at Doncaster in December 1948, the locomotive was also in the autumn of its career; it was withdrawn in January 1964. *Roy Hobbs/Online Transport Archive*

TOP

With the famous Abbey in the background, Raven-designed Class Q6 No 63393 is seen on shed at Whitby on 20 September 1962. By the early 1960s, although the line north from Whitby West Cliff had closed, it was still possible to reach the town from three directions: along the coast from Scarborough, from the west from Middlesbrough and from the south via Pickering. If the Beeching report had been carried out to the full, all three lines would have lost their passenger services. As it was, the line from Middlesbrough was retained and the section of the line south was preserved from Grosmont to Pickering as the North Yorkshire Moors Railway. Courtesy of the preserved line, steam services once again regularly reach the town. No 63393 was one of 120 of this North Eastern Railway design to be built between 1913 and 1921; all were withdrawn by the end of 1966 with No 63395 being preserved. *Neil Davenport/Online Transport Archive*

MIDDLE

Class A4 No 60010 *Dominion of Canada* awaits departure from King's Cross station with the 1.15pm service to Leeds one day during March 1963. Following withdrawal in May 1965, No 60010 was slated for scrapping — indeed certain parts were removed — but the locomotive survived at the end of a siding in Darlington until being rescued for cosmetic restoration in 1966. Donated initially to the Canadian Railroad Historical Association, No 60010 has been based in Canada ever since except for a brief return to the UK in 2012/13 when all six surviving members of the class were reunited to mark the 75th anniversary of Mallard's record-breaking run. *Roy Hobbs/ Online Transport Archive*

BOTTOM

A total of 15 Class Q7 0-8-0s were constructed at Darlington Works to a design by Raven. The first five were completed in 1919 and the final 10 five years. Designed primarily for coal traffic, the entire class remained in service until the end of 1962 when all were withdrawn. The first of the class to be completed, No 63460, was acquired for preservation after withdrawal. It is seen here on 28 September 1963, after preservation, at the head of the joint Railway Correspondence & Travel Society/Stephenson Locomotive Society 'North Eastern' rail tour of 28 September 1963 passing the shed at Consett. *Roy Hobbs/Online Transport Archive*

Recorded on the Silksworth Colliery branch in September 1967 — towards the end of its working life — is Class J27 No 65894. This was one of 115 0-6-0s built to a design of Worsdell for the North Eastern Railway of which 80 were constructed at Darlington between April 1906 and August 1908 whilst the final 35 — of which No 65894 was the last to be completed — were built to Raven's slightly modified design at Darlington between November 1921 and September 1923. No 65894, one of the last to survive, was to be preserved on withdrawal. *Roy Hobbs/ Online Transport Archive*

On 30 September 1963, and part of the same RCTS/SLS tour, Ivatt-designed 2-6-0 No 43129 approaches Guisborough station with the special. The locomotive was one of a class of 162 built at Darlington, Doncaster and Horwich works between December 1947 and September 1952. When originally designed, the locomotives featured double chimneys; this was not a success, however, and the design was modified to feature a single blastpipe and chimney and later locomotives were built as modified from new. No 43129 was completed at Horwich in November 1951. The branch from Nunthorpe to Guisborough lost its passenger services on 2 March 1964 and closed completely six months later. *Roy Hobbs/Online Transport Archive*

Alnwick Castle is the home of the Duke of Northumberland and, as a result, the railway station that served the town was much grander than the short branch from Alnmouth would normally have merited. Although the three-mile branch opened originally in 1850, the station illustrated in the background dated to 1887 when the North Eastern Railway branch from Alnwick to Cornhill opened. However, passenger services over the Cornhill route ceased in 1930 and closed completely between Alnwick and Ilderton in March 1953. On 18 June 1966 — the last day of steam operation over the branch — Thompson-designed Class K1 2-6-0 No 62011 is pictured departing with a service towards Alnmouth. Despite opposition, passenger services from Alnwick were withdrawn on 29 January 1968 and the line closed completely nine months later. *Roy Hobbs/Online Transport Archive*

LONDON MIDLAND
R E G I O N

The London Midland Region, which adopted maroon as its corporate colour, comprised all of the lines previously operated in England and Wales by the LMS. As such it included the routes owned at the Grouping by the Furness, Maryport & Carlisle, Midland (including the London, Tilbury & Southend acquired in 1912), London & North Western (including the Lancashire & Yorkshire taken over in 1922), North London and North Staffordshire railways. Apart from the major main lines to the north – the West Coast and Midland main lines – the LMR also included significant operations in North and South Wales, reaching as far west as Holyhead and Swansea, and in the East Midlands, where the London & North Western had reached Peterborough and the Midland had reached Lincoln. The first significant inter-regional transfer occurred in 1949 when the Eastern assumed control of the LT&SR route. During the 1950s LMR ceded control of its lines in the East Midlands and South Yorkshire to the Eastern, those in the West and North Ridings to the North Eastern and those in Wales and to the south-west of Birmingham to the Western. In their place, the LMR gained control of the former Great Central main line south from Sheffield through Nottingham and Leicester to London Marylebone as well as the former NER lines in the Tebay area.

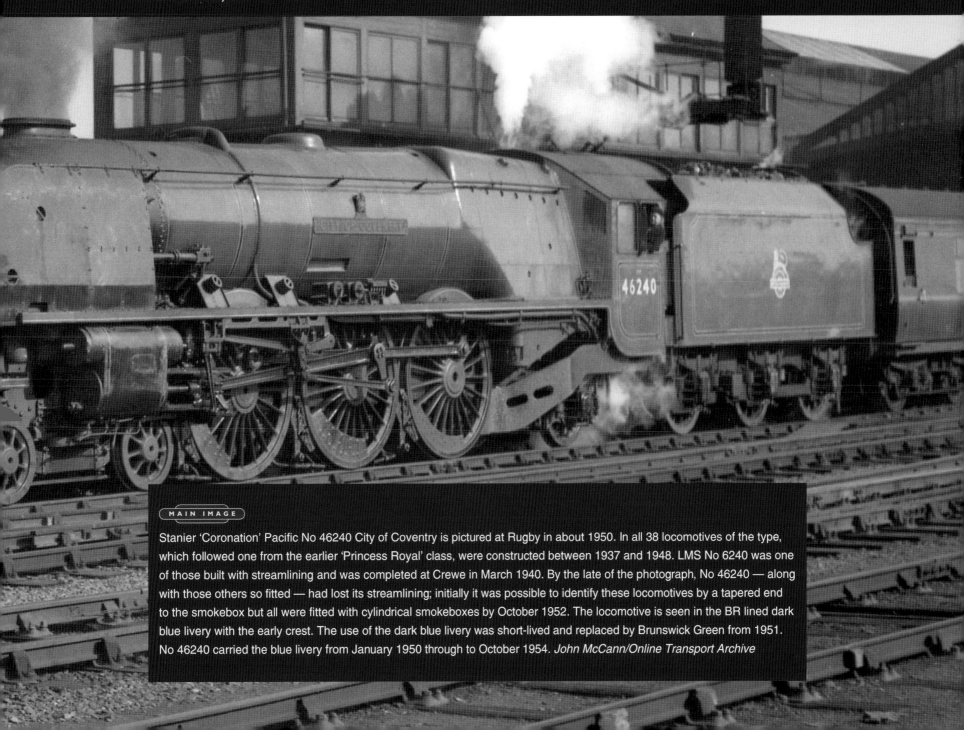

MAIN IMAGE

Stanier 'Coronation' Pacific No 46240 City of Coventry is pictured at Rugby in about 1950. In all 38 locomotives of the type, which followed one from the earlier 'Princess Royal' class, were constructed between 1937 and 1948. LMS No 6240 was one of those built with streamlining and was completed at Crewe in March 1940. By the late of the photograph, No 46240 — along with those others so fitted — had lost its streamlining; initially it was possible to identify these locomotives by a tapered end to the smokebox but all were fitted with cylindrical smokeboxes by October 1952. The locomotive is seen in the BR lined dark blue livery with the early crest. The use of the dark blue livery was short-lived and replaced by Brunswick Green from 1951. No 46240 carried the blue livery from January 1950 through to October 1954. *John McCann/Online Transport Archive*

MAIN IMAGE

Stanier Pacific No 46201 *Princess Elizabeth* is also recorded heading south from Rugby with the Up 'Merseyside Express' in 1952. Built at Crewe in November 1933, No 46201 was the second of Stanier's 'Princess Royal' class to be completed. Destined to survive in service for a further decade, the locomotive was preserved on withdrawal in October 1962. *John McCann/Online Transport Archive*

TOP

On 21 May 1950 rebuilt 'Royal Scot' 4-6-0 No 46119 *Lancashire Fusilier* awaits departure from Chester with the 4.25pm service to Euston. The class was originally designed by Henry Fowler and introduced in 1927 with parallel boilers but the locomotives constructed were rebuilt by William Stanier between 1943 and 1955. The rebuild resulted in the fitting of tapered boilers, double chimneys and, from 1947, smoke deflectors. It is in this guise that No 46119 was recorded; this was one of the class to be rebuilt prior to Nationalisation. No 46119 was to be withdrawn in November 1963; two of the class — Nos 46100 *Royal Scot* and 46115 *Scots Guardsman* — survive in preservation. *Peter N. Williams/Online Transport Archive*

MIDDLE

With water cascading over the tender, demonstrating that the locomotive is picking up water from the troughs, rebuilt 'Royal Scot' No 46138 *The London Irish Rifleman* heads south at Whitmore with an Up service from Liverpool to Euston on 22 July 1951. *Peter N. Williams/Online Transport Archive*

BOTTOM

During the second half of 1951, rebuilt 'Royal Scot' No 46101 *Royal Scots* Grey heads south from Rugby with an Up West Coast main line service towards London Euston. A total of 71 'Royal Scots' were constructed to the design of Fowler between 1927 and 1930; however, in 1943 in Stanier began a programme of rebuilding them with tapered boilers, double chimneys and new cylinders. No 46101 was one of 27 rebuilt before Nationalisation; the remaining 44 were so treated by the end of 1955. *John McCann/Online Transport Archive*

It has clearly just rained, but there is now early autumnal sun as Stanier 'Black Five' 4-6-0 No 45364 passes northbound through Appleby station with a Carlisle-bound service. The Settle & Carlisle line was one of those listed for closure by Beeching; however, although most intermediate stations — but not Appleby — were to close (although many have subsequently reopened) a massive campaign when the route was last threatened in the 1980s saw the line secured for the future. *Neil Davenport/Online Transport Archive*

Bath Green Park was the northern terminus of the Somerset & Joint line south to Bath and was also the terminus of the LMS route from Bristol and the north. From 1927 until 1962, when the service was rerouted to run via Oxford, Bath Green Park saw the famous 'Pines Express — the through train from Manchester to Bournemouth and return — in its platforms but on this occasion the station is occupied by a much more humble service — a two-coach train behind Ivatt-designed 2-6-2T No 41242. At this stage the locomotive was relatively new, having been completed at Crewe Works in September 1949. *R. W. A. Jones/Online Transport Archive*

The short — 1¾ mile — branch to Holywell Town was a relatively late addition to the railway network. The line was opened by the London & North Western from a junction on the Chester to Holyhead line on 1 July 1912. The journey time from Holywell Junction was about eight minutes and, even as late as 1953, there 15 return workings on Mondays to Fridays with 19 on Saturdays. However, the following year BR decided to withdraw the service and the last timetable issued, for the summer of that year, showed only five return workings with 10 Down and nine Up services on Saturdays. The last trains operated on 4 September 1954. This view of the station, looking north, taken shortly before closure shows a one-coach service awaiting departure. *R. W. A. Jones/Online Transport Archive*

Awaiting departure from one of the bay platforms at the southern end of Shrewsbury station is Fowler-designed 2-6-4T No 42305. This was one 125 locomotives built between 1927 and 1934 at Derby Works; No 42305 emerged in January 1928. Shrewsbury was a joint station, seeing services operated by both the London Midland and Western regions and the overall roof was the result an expansion of the station undertaken between 1899 and 1903. The last of the 2-6-4Ts was withdrawn by the end of 1966; the overall roof had, by that date, also disappeared, being dismantled during 1964. *R. W. A. Jones/Online Transport Archive*

The Stanier 'Black Five' class was to be one of the single largest types of steam locomotive ever constructed for operation on Britain's railways. Constructed over some 16 years, more than 840 of this mixed traffic 4-6-0 were built. No 45004, seen here near Harrow on 18 August 1956, was one of the earliest of the class to be completed, being constructed at Crewe Works in March 1935. The first of the type to be built, No 45000, was to be preserved on withdrawal in October 1967 and a further 16 examples of the class also survive in preservation. *Neil Davenport/Online Transport Archive*

Seen near Watford on 19 March 1955 is 'Britannia' class Pacific No 70044 *Earl Haig* with the Up 'Mancunian' service towards London Euston. At this date the locomotive was less than two years old — having been completed at Crewe Works in June 1953 — but its life was to be relatively short. It was one of 11 of the class to be taken out of service during 1966. The 'Mancunian' was to operate on the West Coast main line from 1927; it too failed to survive beyond the end of 1966 — a casualty of the route's electrification. *Neil Davenport/Online Transport Archive*

On 8 May 1955 the Railway Correspondence & Travel Society organised a rail tour from Nottingham Midland to Crewe Works; the 'East Midlander' tour was hauled for the bulk of the journey by ex-LNER Class B12 4-6-0 No 61554. The 'B12s' had originally been designed for the Great Eastern by Hill for use on the heavy loaded trains on the main line from Liverpool Street to Harwich. In all, 71 were constructed between 1911 and 1920 with a further 10 following in 1928. A total of 72 remained in service at Nationalisation with a number having been transferred to Scotland to operate on the ex-Great North of Scotland lines. All were withdrawn by the end of 1959 with the exception of No 61572 that soldiered on until September 1961 and was preserved on withdrawal. *John McCann/Online Transport Archive*

Immediately prior to the outbreak of World War 2, the LMS and LNER decided to construct a test plant at Rugby in order to examine the performance of locomotives. Although delayed by the war, the facility opened in 1949 and, over the next decade, more than 25 locomotives underwent a rigorous examination. One of those tested was Stanier Pacific No 46225 *Duchess of Gloucester* — seen here outside the test plant on 23 May 1955. The locomotive had been under test from early January 1955 and work was only completed the week before the photograph was taken. *John McCann/Online Transport Archive*

MAIN IMAGE

Historically there were only two stations on the BR network that possessed platforms serving all lines on all three sides of a triangle. One was at Queensbury, on the now long-closed ex-Great Northern line from Bradford to Halifax or Keighley, and the second — seen here in July 1958 — was at Ambergate in Derbyshire, where the ex-Midland main lines north to Sheffield and north-west to Manchester diverged. Here an unidentified 'Compound' 4-4-0 is seen at the station with a Down local heading towards Sheffield. The Up and Down fast lines bypassed the station on an alignment slightly to the east. Today Ambergate station remains open, but the only platforms to survive are those serving the truncated route to Manchester with traffic on the Derby to Matlock line. *John McCann/Online Transport Archive*

TOP

Recorded at Watford shed during 1947 are No 40672 and 41320. The former was one of 138 '2P' 4-4-0s designed by Fowler for the LMS and constructed between 1928 and 1932. All were to be withdrawn by the end of 1962. The latter was one of 130 2-6-2Ts designed by Ivatt and built between 1946 and 1952. The type was built primarily for cross-country and branch line working. A handful survived into 1967 but all had been withdrawn by the end of that year. Although none of the 4-4-0s survive, four of the Ivatt tanks do remain. Watford shed was to close in March 1965. *Marcus Eavis/Online Transport Archive*

MIDDLE

One of the 30-strong BR Standard Class 2 2-6-2Ts — No 84004 — passes through Bedford St Johns station during 1957 with a westbound service towards Bletchley. Although passenger services were withdrawn from the section from Bedford St Johns to Cambridge on 1 January 1968, passenger services continued to run into Bedford St Johns from Bletchley until May 1984 when they were diverted into Bedford Midland. Although none of the Class 2 2-6-2Ts survived into preservation, one of the similar 2-6-0s — No 78059 — was rescued from the scrapyard at Barry without a tender and is being restored as No 84030, effectively the 31st member of the class. *Marcus Eavis/Online Transport Archive*

BOTTOM

On 28 May 1958 No 46207 *Princess Alice of Connaught* has the road as it powers through Wavertree. This member of Stanier's 'Princess Royal' class was notable for having appeared in the documentary film *A Study in Steel* of 1937 that recorded the locomotive's construction. It was also to be the locomotive hauling the express that was derailed at Weedon on 21 September 1951. The accident, which resulted in 15 fatalities with a further 35 injured, was the result of a faulty bogie on the locomotive. Recovered and restored to service, No 46207 was to survive until November 1961. Two of the class — Nos 46201 *Princess Elizabeth* and 46203 *Princess Mary Rose* — survive in preservation. *John McCann/Online Transport Archive*

MAIN IMAGE

Towards the end of their lives, a number of Stanier's 'Princess Coronation' Pacifics were repainted into maroon. One of those so treated — in August 1960 — was No 46240 *City of Coventry*, which was recorded here at Willesden shed in March 1964. Although more than 20 of the class were still in service at the end of 1963, the decision was taken that the class be eliminated by the end of September 1964 even though a number had only recently been outshopped and were in an excellent condition. Although No 46240 was to be withdrawn for scrap at that time, three of the type — Nos 46229/33/35 — do survive in preservation. *Roy Hobbs/Online Transport Archive*

TOP

On 10 July 1958 rebuilt 'Royal Scot' No 46116 *Irish Guardsman* speeds past Spondon Junction, near Derby, with an Up service on the ex-Midland main line towards St Pancras. No 46116 dated originally to September 1927 when it was completed at North British in Glasgow. Latterly based at Carlisle (Kingmoor) shed, the locomotive was one of more than 20 of the class withdrawn during 1963. *John McCann/Online Transport Archive*

MIDDLE

During 1959, BR used a number Class 9F 2-10-0s on a series of test runs hauling 16 ton mineral wagons on the Midland main line. On 15 March of that year two of the locomotives used — Nos 92153 and 92156 — are seen awaiting departure from Bedford Midland station. Both locomotives were at that stage relatively new, both being completed at Crewe Works in October 1957 (No 92153) and November 1957 (No 92156). One of the consequences of the rapid demise of steam during the 1960s was that both locomotives had very short careers; No 92156 survived until January 1968 but No 92156 succumbed in July 1967. *John McCann/Online Transport Archive*

BOTTOM

Although it is an ex-LNER locomotive operating on ex-LNER service, by 1959, and the date of this view of Class B1 4-6-0 No 61142 heading a down service through Aylesbury station, management of the former Great Central main line north to Leicester and Nottingham had passed to the London Midland Region. On the right can be seen the small two-road engine shed built by the GWR to serve its services from Princes Risborough; this was to close finally in 1962. *Marcus Eavis/Online Transport Archive*

MAIN IMAGE

Pictured breasting Shap Summit on 18 July 1964 is 'Britannia' class Pacific No 70007 *Coeur-de-Lion*. This locomotive, built originally at Crewe in April 1951, was one of the type originally delivered to the Eastern Region. However, the end of Eastern steam towards the end of 1962 saw No 70007 transferred from March shed to Carlisle (Klngmoor). No 70007, withdrawn in June 1965, was destined to be the first of the class to be taken out of service. *Roy Hobbs/Online Transport Archive*

TOP

The BR Standard Class 9F 2-10-0 was designed primarily for heavy freight traffic and was developed from the earlier War Department class. In all 251 locomotives were constructed between 1954 and 1960, many of which saw less than a decade in service before withdrawal. One of the services for which they were noted was the movement of iron ore from the docks at Bidston to the steelworks at Shotton and No 92208 is seen heading south on one of these duties on 8 June 1965. No 92208 was new in June 1959 and survived only until October 1967. *Geoff Smith/Online Transport Archive*

MIDDLE

One of the facets of railway operation on a number of heavily graded lines — such as the West Coast main line — was the necessity of providing banking locomotives to the rear of heavy passenger and freight trains as they ascended the gradient. On 3 July 1965 Fairburn-designed 2-6-4T No 42225 is providing assistance for a car carrier loaded with Ford Anglias as the train ascends towards Shap with a northbound service. No 42225 was originally built at Derby in April 1946 and would survive almost exactly 20 years in service before withdrawal in June 1966. *Roy Hobbs/Online Transport Archive*

BOTTOM

On the same day, 'Jubilee' class No 45721 *Impregnable* has just completed the long climb to Shap and is now descending south from the summit with an Up service. The yellow stripe on the cab side was to indicate that the locomotive was not permitted to travel south of Crewe on the lines that had recently been electrified to 25kV. By this date, No 45721 had been in service for almost 30 years; it was not to survive much longer, however, as it was withdrawn two months later. *Roy Hobbs/Online Transport Archive*

MAIN IMAGE

On 26 August 1966, 'Jubilee' class No 45697 *Achilles* makes
an impressive sight as it crosses the majestic Ribblehead
Viaduct with an early morning freight heading for Carlisle.
The 24-span viaduct extends for about quarter of a mile and,
with construction commencing in October 1870, was finally
opened in August 1875. It was the condition of the viaduct that
was one factor in BR seeking to close the Settle & Carlisle
line in the 1980s; however, following a vociferous campaign
the line was reprieved and the viaduct has since undergone
much restoration and refurbishment work. *Roy Hobbs/Online
Transport Archive*

TOP

Pictured heading eastbound along the ex-LNWR main line
from Holyhead to Chester at Llandulas with an up service
is one of the ubiquitous 'Black Five' class, No 45429. This
particular example of the class was constructed by Armstrong
Whitworth and new in November 1937; by the date of the
photograph, No 45429 was approaching the end of its career
— it was to be withdrawn the following month. *Geoff Smith/
Online Transport Archive*

MIDDLE

Recorded on the climb up to the summit at Copy Pit, on the
route from Todmorden to Burnley, in May 1966 is Stanier-
designed 'Jubilee' No 45647 *Sturdee* with a service from
Leeds to Blackpool. Built originally at Crewe in January 1935,
No 45647 was one of eight of the class to survive into 1967,
with all withdrawn by the end of that year. Four survive in
preservation. *Roy Hobbs/Online Transport Archive*

BOTTOM

On the same day, Stanier 'Black Five' 4-6-0 No 45363
approaches Ais Gill summit with an Up van train heading south
towards Skipton and Leeds. The summit at Ais Gill — 1,168ft
above sea level — is the highest point on the scenic Settle &
Carlisle line. *Roy Hobbs/Online Transport Archive*

MAIN IMAGE

It's 1 August 1968 and main-line steam has only days to go as BR Standard Class 4MT No 75048 is pictured at Silverdale, on the former Furness Railway, with a southbound freight towards Carnforth. No 75048, built at Swindon in October 1953, was one of the 80 strong class. *Roy Hobbs/Online Transport Archive*

TOP

As the end of steam approached, there were inevitable a large number of specials operated. On the actual last day of normal timetabled services — 4 August 1968 — 'Black Five' No 45156 was used on a special — seen here near Gisburn — on a special from Stockport via Hellifield to Carnforth and return. No 45156 had originally been named *Ayrshire Yeomanry* — one of only five of the type to be named in BR days and was the last of the quintet — albeit now lacking its nameplates — to remain in service. The final 'Fifteen Guinea' special was to operate exactly a week later. *Roy Hobbs/Online Transport Archive*

BOTTOM

By 1967 the number of Stanier-designed 'Jubilee' class 4-6-0s remaining in service had been reduced to single figures and by the date of this photograph — 10 July 1967 — only three were still operational. No 45697 *Achilles* looks in reasonable external condition — albeit shorn of its nameplates — whilst awaiting its next duty at Leeds Holbeck shed. No 45697 was to be withdrawn in September 1967, leaving No 45593 *Kolhapur* (subsequently preserved) and No 45562 *Alberta* to survive until October 1967 and November 1967 respectively. *Roy Hobbs/ Online Transport Archive*

SCOTTISH REGION

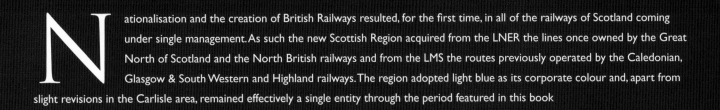

Nationalisation and the creation of British Railways resulted, for the first time, in all of the railways of Scotland coming under single management. As such the new Scottish Region acquired from the LNER the lines once owned by the Great North of Scotland and the North British railways and from the LMS the routes previously operated by the Caledonian, Glasgow & South Western and Highland railways. The region adopted light blue as its corporate colour and, apart from slight revisions in the Carlisle area, remained effectively a single entity through the period featured in this book

MAIN IMAGE

Two ex-LNER locomotives — 'B12' 4-6-0 No 61532 (one of the members of the ex-GER design to be sent to Scotland to operate over the ex-Great North of Scotland system) and 'V2' 2-6-0 No 60898 — depart from Aberdeen with a southbound service towards Dundee in about 1951. *John McCann/Online Transport Archive*

MAIN IMAGE

Standing at Perth station is Ivatt-designed No 46464. This was one of 128 2-6-0s built between December 1946 and March 1953 to the design. Ivatt designed this and a similar 2-6-2T as lightweight locomotives for use on cross-country and branch line services. Mostly based on the London Midland Region and Scottish regions, a number were also employed on the Eastern, North Eastern and Western regions. Built at Crewe in June 1950 — the last of the type to be built there — No 46464 was allocated to Dundee (Tay Bridge) for many years and was one of seven of the type to be preserved on withdrawal. *R. W. A. Jones/Online Transport Archive*

TOP

One of the 4-4-0s designed by Pickersgill for the Caledonian Railway, No 54493, stands on the turntable at Inverness shed. This was one of 48 locomotives of the type; they were built at St Rollox Works as well as by North British and Armstrong Whitworth. No 54493 was one of these built by Armstrong Whitworth and was new in May 1921. The shed at Inverness was opened by the Highland Railway and eventually comprised three-quarters of a round house; closed in June 1961, the building was demolished by the end of 1963. *R. W. A. Jones/Online Transport Archive*

MIDDLE

Standard 4MT 2-6-4T No 80029, fitted with a snowplough, makes a dramatic departure as it heads southwards from Aberdeen. The locomotive was completed at Brighton in January 1952 and was this virtually brand new when recorded in this view. A total of 155 of the class were built between July 1951 and March 1957; with the rundown of steam, a number of the class survived in service for less than a decade. No 80029 was to achieve 13 years' operation before withdrawal in December 1965. The type is well represented in preservation, with no fewer than 15 surviving the cutters' torch. *John McCann/Online Transport Archive*

BOTTOM

During July 1955 ex-Caledonian Railway Class 439 0-4-4T No 55221 stands at Lossiemouth station awaiting its return working towards Elgin on the ex-Great North of Scotland Railway branch. Designed by McIntosh, 78 of the class were constructed at St Rollox Works between March 1900 and November 1922, the last 10 being completed to a slightly modified design by Pickersgill. All bar two were inherited by BR in 1948. More than half — including No 55221 — were still in service at the end of 1960 but all had been withdrawn by the end of 1962. One of the class — No 55189 — survives in preservation. The Lossiemouth branch was to lose its passenger services on 6 April 1964 and to close completely on 28 March 1966. *John McCann/Online Transport Archive*

Pictured at Boat of Garten, on the line from Craigellachie to
Aviemore, on 22 May 1956, another 'D49' No 6226 is pictured
with the 8.30am freight from Elgin. The pick-up freight calling
at most wayside stations was a feature of the traditional
railway in an era when British Railways was still designated
as the 'common carrier'. A number of marshalling yards —
such as Millerhill in Edinburgh — were constructed during the
late 1950s and early 1960s in order to handle the traffic that
these trains generated; however, deemed largely uneconomic
in Beeching's report, the pick-up freight was to disappear
alongside main-line steam and render many of the new
marshalling yards redundant. *John McCann/Online Transport
Archive*

On 31 July 1955 Gresley-designed Class A3 No 60097
Humorist makes an impressive sight as it departs from
Aberdeen with a service towards Dundee and Edinburgh.
No 60097 was one of the early examples of Gresley's 'A3'
design to be completed — being completed at Doncaster
Works in early 1929 — and at this date was still fitted with
only a single chimney; it was modified with a double chimney
in 1957. A Scottish Region locomotive when pictured here, it
was withdrawn from Edinburgh's St Margaret's shed in August
1963. *John McCann/Online Transport Archive*

Knockando station was one of the intermediate stations on the
ex-Great North of Scotland Railway route from Craigellachie
to Boat of Garten. Here Pickersgill-designed Class D40 4-4-0
No 62277 *Gordon Highlander* stands at the station with an
eastbound service towards Craigellachie. A total of 21 of this
class of locomotive were built by the GNoSR between 1899
and 1915 of which 18 survived to Nationalisation. No 62277
was destined to be the last of the class to survive; withdrawn in
1958, the locomotive was restored as GNoSR No 49 — one of
a quartet of Scottish locomotives restored to their original livery
at the time — and with the other three operated specials for a
number of years. It is now preserved in the Glasgow Museum
of Transport. *John McCann/Online Transport Archive*

On 27 March 1959 an unidentified Class 4 2-6-0 approaches
Leuchars Junction station from the south. The station served
the East Coast main line as well as the branches towards
St Andrews southwards and Tayport to the north. However,
by the date of this photograph passenger services had been
withdrawn on the line to Tayport — on 9 January 1956 —
although the short section serving the original station at
Leuchars — Old — remained for freight traffic. Although
the section from St Andrews south to Leven closed on 6
September 1965, passenger services to the university city
itself were not finally withdrawn until 6 January 1969. *John
McCann/Online Transport Archive*

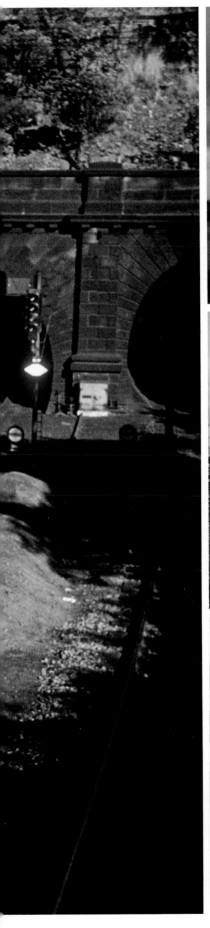

Thompson-design 'A2/3' Pacific No 60518 *Tehran* — named after a racehorse rather than the capital of Iran — is pictured running light engine through Princes Gardens in Edinburgh on 29 July 1961. As CME of the LNER, Edward Thompson planned the construction of two classes of Pacific locomotive; the 'A2s' were designed to be equally capable on both passenger and freight duties. In all, Thompson received sanction for the construction of 43 'A2s', but — following his retirement — only 15 were completed; his successor modified the design for the final 15 completed. No 60518 was completed at Doncaster in December 1946; it was one of six withdrawn in November 1962. The remainder were all withdrawn by June 1965; none were preserved. *Ian Dunnet/ Online Transport Archive*

With the city of Dundee in the background, an unidentified Class A3 Pacific heads southbound across the Tay Bridge — the longest railway bridge in Britain — with an Up fish train heading into Fife on 27 March 1959. The remains of the piers from the original Tay Bridge, designed by Sir Thomas Bouch, which collapsed in a gale in December 1879, are not visible in this view but can normally be seen slightly to the east of the replacement viaduct. *John McCann/Online Transport Archive*

On 15 May 1959 ex-Caledonian Railway Class 3P No 54493 departs from Inverness with a service one the Highland line towards Muir of Ord. This was one of 48 Pickersgill 4-4-0s — Nos 54461-45408 — inherited by BR in 1948 that were constructed by Armstrong Whitworth, North British and the railway itself at St Rollox Works between 1916 and 1922. All were withdrawn by the end of 1962; No 54493 succumbing in the November of the previous year. *Paul de Beer/Online Transport Archive*

The second BR Class 4 2-6-0 No 76001, completed at Horwich in December 1952, skirts the southern shore of Loch Linnhe on 20 July 1960 as it approaches the original terminus at Fort William. The terminus here was opened by the North British Railway on 7 August 1894 but the line was cut back slightly by British Rail when the new station was opened on 13 June 1975. Today, Fort William is again a regular destination for steam trains as tourist services to and from Mallaig — now known as the 'Jacobite' — operate from the station each summer until late October. Although steam was originally withdrawn over the route in 1967, the 'Jacobite' and its predecessors have now been operating annually for more than 30 years, providing additional revenue to this remote route. *Ian Dunnet/Online Transport Archive*

MAIN IMAGE

Pictured at the ex-Caledonian Railway terminus at Blairgowrie on 23 April 1962 is Pickersgill-designed 4-4-0 No 54465 which had arrived at the station hauling the joint Branch Line Society and Stephenson Locomotive Society 'Scottish Rambler' railtour. A total of 48 of the type were inherited by BR in 1948 but only eight were to remain in service at the start of 1962 with the last being withdrawn at the end of that year. Although the station looks intact at this stage, regular passenger services over the branch from Coupar Angus had already been withdrawn — on 10 January 1955 — and the line was to close completely on 6 December 1965. *Roy Hobbs/Online Transport Archive*

TOP

The penultimate Class A1 No 60161 *North British* approaches Edinburgh from the east on 29 July 1961 with a down passenger service. Following on from the conversion of No 60113 *Great Northern*, Arthur Peppercorn designed the 'A1' class along similar lines to his 'A2' class but with larger — 6ft 8in rather than 6ft 2in — driving wheels. A total of 49 were built between August 1948 and December 1949, with construction being split between Darlington and Doncaster works. No 60161 emerged from the latter in December 1949. The 'A1' class was intact until the end of 1961 but thereafter withdrawals saw only two remain operation into 1966; these two survivors were both withdrawn during early 1966. None of the class was preserved at the time but construction of a replica saw No 60163 *Tornado* emerge in 2008. *Ian Dunnet/ Online Transport Archive*

MIDDLE

With the engine shed visible in the background, ex-LMS Class 4F 0-6-0 No 44257 can be seen shunting the yard at Forfar on 23 April 1962. Following the Grouping in 1923, the LMS adopted the Midland Railway's '4F' as its standard freight locomotive and a further 580 of the type were built between 1924 and 1940. No 44257 was completed at Derby in May 1926. The engine shed was finally to close on 18 July 1964. *Roy Hobbs/Online Transport Archive*

BOTTOM

One of the quartet of locomotives restored by the Scottish Region to their original livery, ex-North British 4-4-0 No 256 *Glen Douglas* prepares to pass under the southern approach lines to the Forth Railway Bridge. The locomotive is heading back to rejoin the East Coast main line following a trip on the South Queensferry branch during the joint Branch Line Society/Stephenson Locomotive Society 'Scottish Rambler' railtour on 13 April 1963. *Roy Hobbs/Online Transport Archive*

MAIN IMAGE

On 18 April 1965 the Stephenson Locomotive Society and Branch Line Society organised a tour from Glasgow via Edinburgh and the Waverley route to Carlisle and then returning via the West Coast main line to Glasgow Central. The locomotive selected for the excursion was 'A4' Pacific No 60031 *Golden Plover* which is seen here with the train heading southbound at Galashiels. Although the Waverley route was to be closed in 1969, having been scheduled for closure by the Beeching report, services were restored to a new station — Tweedbank — just south of Galashiels in September 2015. The official first train was hauled by another of the 'A4' class, the preserved No 60009 *Union of South Africa*. *Roy Hobbs/ Online Transport Archive*

TOP

Between Berwick and Edinburgh, the East Coast main line was constructed by the North British Railway and the line is more heavily graded than that south of the border. Seen ascending the 1 in 96 climb at Cockburnspath on 14 April 1963 is 'B1' class 4-6-0 61324 with the southbound joint Branch Line Society/Stephenson Locomotive Society 'Scottish Rambler' railtour to Berwick. *Roy Hobbs/Online Transport Archive*

MIDDLE

The branch from Newton Stewart to Whithorn, which had been part of the Portpatrick & Wigtownshire Joint before the Grouping in 1923, was one of the lines that lost its regular passenger service relatively early in the BR era — on 25 September 1950 — but was to retain its railway line for freight traffic until October 1964. On 15 April 1963, one of the Dugald Drummond-designed 0-6-0s — No 57375 — stands at Whithorn having provided the motive power for a joint Branch Line Society/Stephenson Locomotive Society excursion over the route. *Roy Hobbs/Online Transport Archive*

BOTTOM

St Margarets was the main steam depot for services to and from Edinburgh Waverley and, on 18 April 1965, two classic ex-LNER locomotives await their next duty at the shed. In the distance is 'B1' class No 61345 whilst closer to the camera is 'V2' No 60846. The shed was finally to close on 1 May 1967; subsequently demolished, part of the site is now occupied by Murrayfield stadium. *Roy Hobbs/Online Transport Archive*

Pictured heading southbound from Killin to Killin Junction on the ex-Caledonian Railway branch line is BR Standard 2-6-4T No 80092. By this date the branch was approaching the end of its life; scheduled for closure in the Beeching report, services ended less than three months after the date of this photograph on 28 September 1965. *Roy Hobbs/Online Transport Archive*

Pictured outside Perth shed in July 1965 are Class A4 No 60006 *Sir Ralph Wedgewood* and BR Standard Class 5 4-6-0 No 73145. Following their withdrawal from the crack East Coast main line express services, a number of Sir Nigel Gresley's classic streamlined Pacifics had an Indian Summer operating on services from Glasgow to Aberdeen via the ex-Caledonian Railway main line through Forfar. This was not, however, to last for long and the final examples of the class were withdrawn during the summer of 1966. *Roy Hobbs/Online Transport Archive*

MAIN IMAGE

The old and new order are seen at St Margarets on 19 April 1965. On the left is 'B1' class 4-6-0 No 61396 whist the latter is represented by two English Electric Type 4s — later Class 40 — diesel-electrics. Completed at North British in February 1952, No 61396 was one of seven of the class built that year, the last locomotives constructed by BR to a design inherited from the LNER. *Roy Hobbs/Online Transport Archive*

ABOVE

Amongst the quartet of pre-Grouping locomotives restored by the Scottish Region was Caledonian Railway No 123. This 4-2-2 was a one-off built by the Glasgow-based company Nielsen & Co as en exhibition locomotive in 1886; acquired by the Caledonian, it was to pass to the LMS in 1923. By the date of its withdrawal in 1935 it was the last single-wheeled express locomotive still in service. Preserved on withdrawal, it was restored to operational condition as No 123 in 1958. It is seen here on 19 April 1965 climbing the 1 in 80 gradient on the approach to Cleland during the joint Branch Line Society and Stephenson Locomotive Society railtour. No 123 is now preserved as a static exhibit in Glasgow. *Roy Hobbs/Online Transport Archive*

MAIN IMAGE

Following the end of their work on the East Coast main line, a number of the surviving Class A4 Pacifics had an Indian Summer operating on the ex-LMS main line from Glasgow to Edinburgh — the so-called 'Three Hour Express' — until their final withdrawal. Seen approaching Stirling with a down service towards Aberdeen on 7 May 1966 is No 60034 *Lord Faringdon*. By this date the type's swansong was drawing to a close; No 60034 was finally to be withdrawn three months later. *Roy Hobbs/Online Transport Archive*

TOP

On 8 July 1965 Class V2 2-6-2 No 60835 clears Whitrope Summit, passing the signalbox, with an Up freight from Edinburgh (Millerhill) towards Carlisle. The ex-North British main line south of Hawick traversed sparsely populated areas and the route was scheduled for closure by Beeching, despite the relatively recent investment in a new marshalling yard at Millerhill at its northern end. The route lost its passenger services on 6 January 1969 and closed completely between Hawick and Longtown, just north of Carlisle, at the same time. With the recent successful reopening to Tweedbank, there is now considerable pressure for the restoration of the route through to Carlisle. *Roy Hobbs/Online Transport Archive*

MIDDLE

As elsewhere on the BR network, coal was a significant source of freight revenue for the railway industry in Ayrshire and, on 3 May 1966, ex-LMS 2-6-0 No 42919 is seen approaching Mossblown Junction with a train of coal from Killoch Colliery. No 42919 was one of only two of the class, which originally comprised 245 locomotives built between 1926 and 1932, to survive into 1967. It was withdrawn in April that year. *Roy Hobbs/Online Transport Archive*

BOTTOM

With the Ochil Hills in the background, 'Austerity' 2-8-0 No 90547 heads east from Alloa towards Kincardine with a train load of coal for the power station. During the war some 934 2-8-0s were constructed to a design by Robert Riddles — who was later to oversee the development of the BR Standard designs — for use by the military. Of these 733 were eventually acquired for use by British Railways. Although more than 120 remained in service at the start of 1966, none survived the year and none were to be preserved. However, one of those operated latterly by Swedish Railways was repatriated and preserved. *Roy Hobbs/Online Transport Archive*

MAIN IMAGE

The North British Railway constructed a network of lines to serve Fife; one of these was the Fife Coast line from Thornton Junction via Anstruther and St Andrews to Leuchars Junction. Although passenger services south of St Andrews to Leven were withdrawn on 6 September 1965, freight traffic continued to operate south of Crail and, on 16 June 1966, 'B1' class 4-6-0 Non 61132 heads southbound over the short viaduct at Largo with a short freight. The line from Leven to Crail was to close completely shortly after this photograph was taken, on 18 July 1966. *Roy Hobbs/Online Transport Archive*

TOP

On 28 May 1966. 'Black Five' No 44794 departs from Gleneagles with the 1.30pm 'Three Hour' service from Aberdeen to Glasgow. By this date the branch from Gleneagles west towards Crieff and Comrie had closed, with passenger services ceasing on 6 July 1964 and the line closing completely from Gleneagles to Muthill on that date. *Roy Hobbs/ Online Transport Archive*

BOTTOM

Also on 28 May 1966 sees Gresley-design Class J38 0-6-0 No 65929 heading south towards Alloa on the climb from Tillicoultry with a coal train from Dollar. In all 30 'J38s' were constructed during 1926 at Darlington Works to replace older 0-6-0s inherited in 1923. All were based in Scotland for their operational life, with many seeing service primarily on the lines serving the Fife coalfield. Only three — including No 65929 — survived into 1967 and all were scrapped following withdrawal. *Roy Hobbs/Online Transport Archive*

SOUTHERN
R E G I O N

The Southern Region, which used green as its corporate colour, effectively inherited the lines operated prior to 1948 by the Southern Region. Organisationally, is was divided into three sections: the Eastern (primarily the lines constructed by the South Eastern & Chatham Railway and its predecessors); the Central (the lines inherited from the London, Brighton & South Coast railway and its predecessors) and the Western (those lines built for the London & South Western and its antecedents). As such the Southern stretched from Kent, through the southern home counties and the south coast to Bournemouth, Weymouth and Exeter. Courtesy of the London & South Western Railway's 'Withered Arm', the Southern also initially included lines in Devon and Cornwall serving resorts like Ilfracombe, Bude, Padstow and Wadebridge as well as providing an alternative – inland route via Okehampton – from Plymouth to Exeter. Control of these lines was eventually transferred to the Western Region.

MAIN IMAGE

Pictured with the down 'Golden Arrow' approaching its destination at Dover is 'Britannia' No 70004 *William Shakespeare*. This locomotive, which was built at Crewe and completed in late March 1951, received a special finish for display as part of the Festival of Britain exhibition. As such it was displayed statically on the South Bank between 4 May and 30 September 1951. As part of the BR's involvement for the Festival of Britain, a new rake of 12 Pullman carriages was constructed for the 'Golden Arrow' service from London to Dover for onward travel to Calais and Paris. *D. Kelk/Online Transport Archive*

On 19 April 1954 one of the Maunsell-designed Class U1 2-6-0s built originally for the Southern Railway during 1931 heads westwards through Penshurst station. The signalbox visible on the down platform dated to 1893; this was to survive until 1976. No 31900 — one of the 20-strong class all built at Eastleigh following the rebuilding of an older 2-6-4T in 1928 — was to be withdrawn in December 1962. *Neil Davenport/Online Transport Archive*

On 7 August 1950 'Battle of Britain' class No 34071 *601 Squadron* is pictured at Bickley Junction with the 'Thanet Belle'. At this date the locomotive was just over two years old, having been completed at Brighton Works in April 1948 — one of the first of the type to be built after Nationalisation — and was to be rebuilt in May 1960. The 'Thanet Belle' was a Pullman service introduced by BR in 1948 that linked London Victoria with Broadstairs, Margate and Ramsgate. The service was modified in 1951 and renamed the 'Kentish Belle' but survived only until 1958 when the main line services were electrified. *Peter N. Williams/Online Transport Archive*

It's July 1952 and 'Britannia' class Pacific No 70014 *Iron Duke* — one of those allocated to the Southern Region — makes its way southwards with a down service from Victoria. In the background can be seen the familiar towers of Battersea power station. No 70014 was to remain a Southern Region locomotive until transferred to the London Midland Region in mid-1958. It was to be one of a number of the class withdrawn in late 1967; only one — No 70013 *Oliver Cromwell* (later preserved) — was to survive into the following year. *John McCann/Online Transport Archive*

At Nationalisation in 1948 it was not only the lines controlled by the 'Big Four' that passed into public ownership; a myriad other railways, which had previously escaped being merged, were also acquired. One of these was the Kent & East Sussex line from Robertsbridge to Headcorn. In new ownership, on 15 September 1953, ex-South Eastern Railway No 31065 is pictured at Tenterden Town station. Built originally in 1896 and rebuilt 12 years later, this 0-6-0 was to be preserved following withdrawal in June 1961. *D. Kelk/Online Transport Archive*

MAIN IMAGE

Physically separated from the rest of the railway system, the small network that served the Isle of Wight was still significant, albeit much reduced, in the late 1950s when, on 2 October 1957, one of the ex-LSWR 0-4-4Ts — No W14 *Fishbourne* — used on island services was recorded departing from Ryde Pier Head. Although the majority of the surviving lines on the island were closed in the 1960s, the section from Ryde to Shanklin — electrified using ex-London Underground tube stock — was retained. *Neil Davenport/Online Transport Archive*

TOP

BR Standard 4 2-6-4T No 80033 departs from East Grinstead with a service towards Lewes on 7 May 1955. The ex-London, Brighton & South Coast Railway line south from East Grinstead was initially closed on 13 June 1955 — although the last services actually operated on 29 May 1955 due to an industrial dispute — but a legal challenge resulted in services being restored on 7 August 1956 until formal permission to close was given. The line was closed again on 17 March 1958 but the section between Sheffield Park and Horsted Keynes was leased to the Bluebell Railway — the first section of standard gauge BR line to be preserved — and preserved steam operation commenced in 1960. Following a number of years' work, the Bluebell Railway finally extended its services back to East Grinstead in 2013. *Neil Davenport/Online Transport Archive*

MIDDLE

Viewed from the south, another of the Adams-designed 0-4-4Ts that served on the isle of Wight — No W17 *Ventnor* (appropriately) — is being watered having arrived at Ventnor. The small terminus at Ventnor, which was accessed via a short tunnel set into the hillside visible in the background, was a constrained site and locomotives accessed the run-round loop, on which the locomotive is pictured, via a turntable. *Neil Davenport/Online Transport Archive*

BOTTOM

The 'Golden Arrow' is seen again, this time on 28 March 1959 as 'Merchant Navy' No 35015 *Rotterdam Lloyd* heads through Tonbridge with the down service towards Dover. In all, 30 members of the Bulleid-designed Pacific class entered service between February 1941 and April 1949 but, by the date of the photograph, all had been rebuilt without their air-smoothed casing and with modified valve gear. As rebuilt, the class proved very successful with a third of the class surviving into the last year — 1967 — of Southern Region steam. *Neil Davenport/Online Transport Archive*

MAIN IMAGE

Apart from its main line from Salisbury to Exeter, the Southern
Region operated a number of branch lines on the Devon and
Dorset border. Amongst these was the line from Sidmouth
Junction to Sidmouth and, during 1961, one of the classic
'M7' 0-4-4Ts — No 30024 — is pictured at Tipton St Johns
with a Down service towards Sidmouth. Tipton St Johns was
the junction for the branch to Exmouth via Budleigh Salterton;
this and the line through the station to Sidmouth were both
listed for closure in the Beeching report, with services on both
lines being withdrawn on 6 March 1967. *Marcus Eavis/Online
Transport Archive*

TOP

By 1959, steam operation of the classic 'Golden Arrow'
Pullman service — seen here at Petts Wood behind unrebuilt
'Merchant Navy' No 35028 *Clan Line* — was drawing to a
close. The train become electric-hauled in 1961 but was to
be withdrawn in September 1972 as a result of the decline
in passenger traffic by rail between London and Paris. No
35028 was also to change shortly; it was rebuilt without its
air-smoothed casing and modified valve gear in November
1959; withdrawn in July 1967, No 35028 is one of a number of
the class to survive in preservation. *Peter N. Williams/Online
Transport Archive*

MIDDLE

Viewed from the road over bridge immediately to the east of
the station during the final run-down of main line steam over
the route in 1959, one of the 'Schools' class 4-4-0s heads
towards Bromley South with an Up service. A total of 40 of
the Maunsell-designed class were delivered between March
1930 and July 1935; the class was intact at the end of 1960,
but withdrawal was swift with all being withdrawn by the end of
1962. Three survive in preservation. *Peter N. Williams/Online
Transport Archive*

BOTTOM

With the town of Barnstaple in the background, unrebuilt 'West
Country' No 34035 *Shaftesbury* crosses over the River Taw
with a service from Ilfracombe as it approaches Barnstaple
Junction station. The Barnstaple to Ilfracombe line was
scheduled for closure in the Beeching report with services
being withdrawn on 5 October 1970; although there was an
attempt to preserve the line, this came to nothing and the
viaduct across the river was subsequently demolished. *Marcus
Eavis/Online Transport Archive*

MAIN IMAGE

Heading across the bridge over the River Medina in Newport, on the Isle of Wight, Class O2 0-4-4T No W33 *Bembridge* heads from Newport station with a service from Cowes towards Ryde. Both the surviving routes of the island — from Ryde to Ventnor and to Cowes via Newport — were scheduled for closure in the Beeching report. Passenger services over the section from Ryde St Johns to Cowes ceased on 21 February 1966 although the section from Wootton to Smallbrook Junction has been preserved as the Isle of Wight Steam Railway. The railway bridge in this view has been replaced by a road bridge carrying the dual carriageway Medina Way. *Marcus Eavis/ Online Transport Archive*

ABOVE

Having just got the road during the summer of 1961 Maunsell-designed Class S15 4-6-0 No 30826 makes its departure from Seaton Junction station with an Up service from Exeter to Templecombe. No 30826 was one of 10 locomotives built at Eastleigh between 1927 to Maunsell's modification of the earlier Urie-designed locomotives. Nos 30823-32 incorporated higher boiler pressure and reduced diameter cylinders. Seaton Junction was the junction for the route to Seaton and closed with the branch on 7 March 1966. *Marcus Eavis/Online Transport Archive*

MAIN IMAGE

Long the haunt of the Adams-designed Class 0415 4-4-
2T radial tanks, the Lyme Regis branch underwent some
investment in the late 1950s — sections of track were relaid
and some of the more severe curved eased — to permit the
operation of more modern locomotives. The radial tanks were
displaced by Ivatt-designed 2-6-2Ts, such as No 41307 seen
here at the picturesque terminus in 1961, with one, No 30583,
surviving into preservation. However, the use of the
2-6-2Ts was short-lived as dieselisation came in 1963 but
the line, scheduled for closure in the Beeching report, meant
that these too were not to last long, with the line closing on 29
November 1965. *Marcus Eavis/Online Transport Archive*

ABOVE

Although the Standard Class 9F 2-10-0 was designed primarily
for freight traffic, a number were used on passenger work, most
notably on the Somerset & Dorset Joint line from Bath Green
Park to Bournemouth West. During August 1961, one of the
class — No 92212 (which was eventually preserved) — is seen
heading south from Chilcompton with the 9.35am Saturdays
Only service from Sheffield to Bournemouth. *Roy Hobbs/Online
Transport Archive*

The Hayling Island branch in Sussex saw the final operation of the diminutive Stroudley designed 'Terrier' class 0-6-0T. One of the handful of survivors — No 32646 — is seen awaiting departure from the branch terminus on 27 July 1963, four months before the line closed. This locomotive had originally been built by the London, Brighton & South Coast Railway in 1877 but was sold to the London & South Western in 1903 and operated for some years on the Isle of Wight. Following withdrawal in November 1963, the locomotive was to be preserved, one of 10 of the class to survive. *Roy Hobbs/Online Transport Archive*

Looking in fine external condition — as befitted its status as stand-by locomotive for the royal train — No 32353 was the last of the 17-strong 'K' class 2-6-0 designed by Billinton for the London, Brighton & South Coast Railway to be built. Constructed at Brighton Works in March 1921, the locomotive is seen at Tattenham Corner on Derby Day — 10 June 1962 — awaiting its possible duty for the Up working to Victoria. Although the entire class survived into 1962, all had been withdrawn by the end of the year. *Roy Hobbs/Online Transport Archive*

Over the years a number of locomotives were transferred from main-line duties to departmental work; amongst those so reallocated by the Southern Region were six of the 'USA' class 0-6-0Ts that the Southern Railway purchased in 1946 largely to replace older locomotives in use on the dock railways of Southampton. No DS236 pictured shunting at Lancing Carriage Works on 21 August 1963 had been transferred to departmental stock only four months earlier having been No 30074 prior to that date. Another of the consequences of the decline in the railway network after 1960 was a reduction in the number of workshops required to maintain the fleet; Lancing Carriage Works was one of the casualties and it finally closed on 25 June 1965. With the works closed, No DS236 was withdrawn for scrap; four other examples of the type, however, survive in preservation. *Roy Hobbs/Online Transport Archive*

The footplate crew look forward as they await the road at Basingstoke on 1 August 1964. No 73084 was one of 10 of the Derby-built examples of the BR Standard Class 5MT 4-6-0s allocated to Southern Region to be named — in this case *Tintagel* — as were a further 10 Doncaster-built locomotives. No 73084 was withdrawn in December 1965 for scrap although sister No 73082 *Camelot* was to be preserved. *Neil Davenport/ Online Transport Archive*

Pictured in ex-works condition at Eastleigh in October 1964 is unrebuilt 'West Country' Pacific No 34019 *Bideford*. In 1947 this locomotive was one of two of the class — the other being No 34036 *Westward Ho* — that were converted briefly to oil burning. No 34019 was to survive in service until March 1967. *Roy Hobbs/Online Transport Archive*

During the late summer of 1964 rebuilt 'Merchant Navy' No 35001 *Canadian Pacific* stands awaiting departure from London Waterloo station with the 10.30am service to Bournemouth. The locomotive, the first of Bulleid's revolutionary design to be completed by the Southern Railway in April 1941, was rebuilt in August 1959. *Marcus Eavis/Online Transport Archive*

On 28 March 1965 a rebuilt 'West Country' Pacific skirts Holes Bay with a Down service from Bournemouth to Bournemouth. *Roy Hobbs/Online Transport Archive*

Designed primarily for intermediate passenger and cross-country use, the 115-strong BR Standard Class 4 2-6-0s were constructed at Horwich and Doncaster works between December 1952 and October 1957. One of those allocated to the Southern Region — No 76062 — is seen leaving Salisbury, having just passed through the tunnel to the east of the station, with an up service on 23 May 1965. *Roy Hobbs/Online Transport Archive*

Pictured climbing Medstead Bank heading west from Alton on 9 January 1966, 'S15' No 30837 — one of five built at Eastleigh in 1927 with smaller six-wheel tenders for operation over the Southern's Central section — heads the Locomotive Club of Great Britain 'S15 Farewell' railtour. This was a duplicate service run to cater for demand a week earlier than the originally-promoted tour (which ran on 16 January). By the dates of the tours, No 30837 had actually been withdrawn — in September 1965 — as one of the six of the class to survive into 1965. A total of seven 'S15s' — but not No 30837 — survive in preservation whilst the route west from Alton to Alresford also remains, now operating as the Mid-Hants Railway. *Roy Hobbs/Online Transport Archive*

Rebuilt 'Merchant Navy' Pacific No 35029 *Ellerman Lines* approaches Battledown flyover at Worting Junction on 5 September 1965. Withdrawn a year later, in September 1966, No 35029 was one of the class to be sold for scrap to the famous Woodham Bros scrapyard at Barry. Acquired by the National Railway Museum, the locomotive was sectioned for display in the York museum. No fewer than nine other examples of this 30-strong class also survive in preservation. *Roy Hobbs/Online Transport Archive*

Pacifics — 'West Country' No 34006 *Bude* and 'Battle of Britain' No 34057 *Biggin Hill* — look in fine condition as they approach Winsor Hill tunnel with the Locomotive Club of Great Britain 'Somerset & Dorset Farewell' railtour. The cross-country line from Bath to Bournemouth was one of the most significant closures foreshadowed by the Beeching report. *Roy Hobbs/ Online Transport Archive*

Two of Bulleid's Pacifics make an impressive sight as they head westbound on the through lines at Winchfield station on 30 April 1966. Leading the pair is unrebuilt 'West Country' No 34101 *Lapford* whilst following is a rebuilt 'Battle of Britain' No 34087 *145 Squadron*. The latter had been rebuilt in December 1960. Both locomotives were to survive through to the end of Southern Region steam in July 1967. *Neil Davenport*

MAIN IMAGE

It's 1 April 1967 and rebuilt 'West Country' No 34108
Wincanton draws the attention of two youthful enthusiasts.
By this date Southern Region steam had barely three months
left but No 34108, rebuilt as late as April 1961, was not to
survive until then, being withdrawn the previous month. *Neil
Davenport/Online Transport Archive*

TOP

Pictured from the east side of the castle, BR Standard 4 2-6-0
No 76010 — one of 115 of the type constructed — heads
across the short bridge over the B4351 as a down service from
Wareham approaches Corfe Castle station with a service to
Swanage. Although not scheduled for closure in the Beeching
report, services on the Swanage branch were withdrawn on 3
January 1972. The line was, after track removal, secured for
preservation and once again it is now possible to enjoy steam
operation through this attractive location. *Marcus Eavis/Online
Transport Archive*

BOTTOM

Standing at the east end of Bournemouth station with the
11.25am service to Waterloo is rebuilt 'West Country' No
34013 *Okehampton* during the late summer of 1966. No 34013
— rebuilt in October 1967 and one of the first of the type to
be so treated — was to survive through until July 1967 and
the end of Southern steam. *Marcus Eavis/Online Transport
Archive*

WESTERN REGION

T he Western Region, effectively a continuation of the operational area of the Great Western Railway, stretched from London to the West Country, South Wales and through Oxford, Birmingham, Wolverhampton and Shrewsbury to Birkenhead and Merseyside. Adopting brown as its corporate colour, the Western Region eventually came to encompass the lines of the Southern Region in Devon and Cornwall as well as those of the London Midland Region in South Wales. Control of the main line north of Banbury and the network of lines in the West Midlands was, however, ceded to the London Midland Region.

MAIN IMAGE

Only two narrow gauge branch lines survived to pass into BR ownership; one of these was the ex-Cambrian line from Welshpool to Llanfair Caereinion, which was, by Nationalisation, freight only. The line's motive power was provided by two 0-6-0Ts — Nos 822 The Earl and 823 The Countess — that were built originally by Beyer Peacock in 1902 but were reboilered in 1930 whilst owned by the GWR. On 26 June 1954 the latter is pictured at Welshpool prior to working an enthusiast special up to Llanfair. The line was finally to close on 5 November 1956 but the section from Llanfair to Welshpool (Raven Square) was progressively reopened by preservationists from 1963 onwards and both Nos 822 and 823 survive to operate on the preserved line. *John McCann/Online Transport Archive*

MAIN IMAGE

Almost a decade after Nationalisation, this view of the shed at Swindon on 6 May 1956 sees a locomotive still sporting the initials 'GW' on its tender. Present at this time were a number of ex-GWR 4-6-0 designs, including a 'Hall' and 'Castle' class No 5069 *Isambard Kingdom Brunel*. The shed at Swindon, located on the east side of the line towards Gloucester, was initially opened in 1871 but was significantly extended in both 1892 and 1908. It ceased to accommodate steam locomotives in October 1964. *John McCann/Online Transport Archive*

TOP

On 14 May 1950, ex-GWR 2-6-0 No 9300 heads east through Wellington in Shropshire with an Up freight towards Birmingham. This locomotive was one of 20 built in early 1932 to an older Churchward design modified by Collett. Between 1956 and 1959 all were modified and renumbered, with No 9300 becoming No 7322 in April 1957. All of the 20 were withdrawn by the end of 1959. In the background two ex-GWR tank locomotives stand alongside the small three-road engine shed that was situated on the north side of the station; this was to close in August 1964 and was subsequently demolished. *Peter N. Williams/Online Transport Archive*

MIDDLE

The Great Western Railway's terminus in Birkenhead — Woodside — was opened on 31 March 1878 and possessed five platforms. A somewhat cramped site — it was situated to the north of a short tunnel and adjacent to the ferry terminal — the station was the northern terminus for through services from London Paddington via Birmingham, Wolverhampton and Shrewsbury. Pictured at the station in 1950 is one the large 2-6-2Ts, No 4120, developed by Collett from an earlier Churchward design. Closure of the station was recommended by Beeching in 1963 with all main-line traffic from the north-west due to be concentrated on the electrified West Coast main line. Woodside was finally to close on 5 November 1967 and was subsequently demolished. *John McCann/Online Transport Archive*

BOTTOM

The GWR possessed two types of Collett-designed 0-4-2T primarily for branch line passenger work. The numerically larger of the two classes was the '14xx', which were fitted with equipment to work auto-trains, and the smaller was the 20-strong '58xx' class that was not auto-fitted. One of the latter — No 5810 — is seen at the ex-GWR station in Blaenau Ffestiniog with a service towards Bala Junction in early July 1950. All of the '58xx' class were built at Swindon in 1933 but the type was destined to have a shorter life than many of the '14xx' type; all were withdrawn by the end of September 1959. Passenger services from Blaenau Ffestiniog to Bala ceased on 2 January 1960 and the line closed completely on 27 January 1961. The short section from Blaenau to Trawsfynydd reopened in 1964, following the construction of a connection to the ex-LNWR branch in Blaenau, in order to serve the new nuclear power station. This section was closed once again with the closure of the power station but is the subject of a preservation scheme. *Peter N. Williams/Online Transport Archive*

During 1958, one of the Collett-designed Class 61xx 2-6-2Ts, No 6117, is seen at the head of a service from Aylesbury to Princes Risborough. The line, which had its origins in the Wycombe Railway's broad gauge branch, originally opened in 1863 and was converted to standard gauge five years later. No 6117 was one of 70 of the type constructed at Swindon between April 1931 and November 1935 primarily for use on suburban services in the London area; all were withdrawn by the end of 1965 with one example surviving into preservation. *Marcus Eavis/Online Transport Archive*

On 8 July 1956 the London branch of the Railway Correspondence & Travel Society organised the 'Wessex Wyvern' railtour that covered a number of lines in the Weymouth area. Class 57xx 0-6-0PT No 4624 was used on the branch from Melcombe Regis to Easton and return and the train is seen here at Easton. By this date the branch was freight only, passenger services having been withdrawn on 3 March 1952. *John McCann/Online Transport Archive*

Heading northbound through High Wycombe station on the Great Western & Great Central Joint line on 6 August 1957 is 'Hall' class 4-6-0 No 5983 *Henley Hall* at the head of a train of tanks containing Guinness. *Peter N. Williams/Online Transport Archive*

For a number of the years the Talyllyn Railway Preservation Society — saviour of the narrow famous Welsh narrow gauge railway — sponsored special trains along the ex-Cambrian Railways route to Towyn (now Tywyn). On 27 September 1958 the special is seen at Welshpool behind 'Dukedog' No 9018. The 29-strong class was built at Swindon between 1936 and 1939 to a design of Collett utilising the boilers from the older 'Duke' class allied to outside frames reused from members of the 'Bulldog' class. By 1959 only six of the type remained and all had been withdrawn by the year. One — No 9017 — survives in preservation. *John McCann/Online Transport Archive*

The following year, on 26 September 1959, the Talyllyn special was hauled by two of the 'Dukedog' class — Nos 9004 and 9014 — and the train is seen here following arrival at Towyn. *Paul de Beer/Online Transport Archive*

The branch from Taunton to Barnstaple gave the Great Western access to north Devon and, on 3 June 1961, Churchward-designed '43xx' 2-6-0 No 7305 is seen at Dulverton, one of the more important intermediate stations on the line, with a westbound service. Although the ex-GWR terminus in Barnstaple — Victoria — closed on 13 June 1960 when services were transferred to the ex-LSWR Junction station, it was not until 3 October 1966 when services over whole line were withdrawn. *Marcus Eavis/Online Transport Archive*

MAIN IMAGE

As two youthful spectators look on '72xx' 2-8-2T No 7236 heads westbound through St Fagans on the main line to the west of Cardiff towards Swansea. In all 54 of these locomotives were converted at Swindon Works between 1934 and 1937 from 2-8-0Ts. No 7236 had originally been No 5271 and dated originally to April 1926. It was to survive in service until November 1963; one of the type — No 7229 — survives in preservation. *R. W. A. Jones/Online Transport Archive*

ABOVE

The Culm Valley Light Railway linked Hemyock with Tiverton Junction and a '14xx' 04-2T No 1468 is recorded at the picturesque terminus shunting wagons. Although passenger services were still in operation over the branch when the Beeching report was undertaken, it was one of the routes where closure was already under consideration. Passenger services ceased on 9 September 1963 although the line was to remain open for freight for more than a decade, catering for the significant milk traffic generated by the dairy adjacent to the station. No 1468 was not to survive until the line's loss of passenger traffic; it was finally withdrawn in March 1962. *R. W. A. Jones/Online Transport Archive*

Pictured departing from Machen, on the Brecon & Merthyr
line, is Collett-designed 0-6-0 No 2236. The Brecon & Merthyr
line was one of those to lose its passenger service before
the Beeching report — on 31 December 1962 — although
freight traffic through Machen continued after passenger traffic
ceased. No 2236 was one of 120 locomotives constructed to
replace older 0-6-0 designs; the type was built between 1930
and 1948 with No 2236 being completed at Swindon during
October 1944. All were withdrawn by the end of 1965 with one
surviving in preservation. *R. W. A. Jones/Online Transport
Archive\'*

The most powerful class of 4-6-0 designed for the Great
Western was the 30-strong 'King' class designed by Collett.
The class was produced to enable the GWR to reclaim the
prestige of operating the most powerful locomotives in Britain,
which it had lost to Southern's 'Lord Nelson' class. The
locomotives were built to the maximum weight permitted on the
main lines and so were restricted to operation on the ex-GWR
main lines. The first of the class — No 6000 *King George
V* — emerged from Swindon Works in June 1927 with No
6004 *King George III*, pictured here at Cardiff on 6 April 1962,
being completed the following month. The entire class was
to survive through to 1962 but were all withdrawn by the end
of that year as diesel-hydraulics took over main-line services
from Paddington. No 6004 was one of the earlier casualties,
being withdrawn in June 1962. Three of the class — Nos 6000,
6023 *King Edward II* and 6024 *King Edward I* — have been
preserved, the latter two rescued and restored following some
years at the famous Woodham Bros scrapyard at Barry. *Ian
Dunnet/Online Transport Archive*

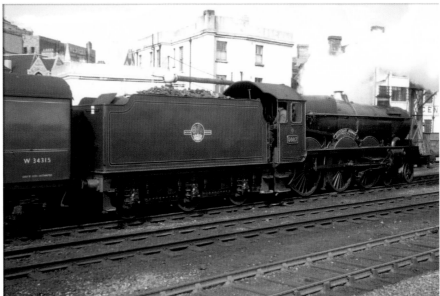

'Castle' class No 5087 *Tintern Abbey* looks in fine external
condition as it awaits departure from Cardiff General (now
Central) with an Up service towards London Paddington on 4
May 1962. The locomotive was completed at Swindon Works
in January 1923 and was to achieve more than 40 years'
service before final withdrawal in August 1963. Although No
5087 was not to survive, eight other members of the class are
still extant. *Ian Dunnet/Online Transport Archive*

The diminutive Class 14xx 0-4-2T was designed by Collett
for use on lightly trafficked branch lines and 75 were built at
Swindon between August 1932 and February 1936. Designed
for operation with autotrains for push-pull services, the class
was seen widely over the Western Region until withdrawals
started in 1956. Many of the lines for which they were
designed were not to survive but one exception is the line from
Bourne End to Marlow, which is still open and was considered
for electrification as part of the Great Western main line project.
Seen at the terminus at Marlow on 8 July 1962 is '14xx' No
1421; this particular locomotive was withdrawn in December
1963 for scrap, although four examples of the type do survive
in preservation. *Roy Hobbs/Online Transport Archive*

MAIN IMAGE

The 27½-mile branch from Whitland to Cardigan had already lost its passenger services by the date of the Beeching report but the line remained open at that time for freight traffic. Passenger services ceased over the route on 10 September 1962 and, shortly before that date, Hawksworth-designed Class 16xx 0-6-0PT No 1643 is seen departing from Kilgerran station with a service towards Cardigan. This class was introduced in October 1949, after Nationalisation, for use for shunting and light branch work. In all, 70 of the type were completed by May 1955 but many had a short life, surviving barely a decade in service as steam was eliminated. All were withdrawn by the end of 1966 with No 1638 being eventually preserved. *R. W. A. Jones/Online Transport Archive*

TOP

Pictured departing from Brecon in the snow of December 1962, Class 57xx 0-6-0PT No 9616 heads an eastbound service towards Talyllyn Junction. More than 770 of this type of tank engine was constructed for the GWR and for the Western Region between 1929 and 1949, making it the single largest class of locomotive that the Western Region inherited from its predecessor. No 9616 was one of the later examples to be completed, being built at Swindon Works in September 1945. By the date of the photograph, passenger services through Brecon were drawing to a close; the line was closed on 31 December 1962. *R. W. A. Jones/Online Transport Archive*

MIDDLE

Amongst the most significant freight traffic generated in Cornwall was china clay. The branch from Bodmin to Wenford Bridge was one of the most important lines that catered for this work and, following the transfer of the Southern Region's 'Withered Arm' network beyond Exeter to the Western Region, 0-6-0PTs replaced in 1962 the venerable Beattie well tanks that had previously operated over the line. On 4 May 1964 one of trio of Collett-designed locomotives transferred to the branch — No 1368 — approaches Dunmere Junction from Wenford Bridge. Six of this type of Pannier Tank were constructed at Swindon in February 1934; sister locomotive No 1369 — another of those transferred in 1962 — survives in preservation. *Roy Hobbs/Online Transport Archive*

BOTTOM

In June 1964 another of the diminutive '14xx' class 0-4-2Ts propels its autocoach with an Up service from Gloucester towards Stroud through the Golden Valley. *Roy Hobbs/Online Transport Archive*

Although timetabled passenger services over the branch from Newnham to Cinderford, in the Forest of Dean, ceased on 3 November 1958, the route remained open for freight traffic. On 20 June 1964 members of the Railway Enthusiasts Club enjoyed a brake van tour of the line and their train, hauled by Hawksworth-design 0-6-0PT No 1658, is pictured at the branch terminus. The line from Bullo Pit to Cinderford was to be closed completely with the withdrawal of freight traffic on 1 August 1967. *Roy Hobbs/Online Transport Archive*

On 10 July 1964 '4575' class 2-6-2T No 5508 approaches West Drayton with a short freight from Uxbridge Vine Street. By this date, passenger services on the short ex-GWR branch to Uxbridge had been withdrawn — on 10 September 1962 — and freight traffic was to cease shortly after the date of this photograph (on 13 July 1964). *Roy Hobbs/Online Transport Archive*

The last wholly new type of 4-6-0 to be developed by the Great Western Railway was the 30-strong 'County' class designed by Hawksworth and built at Swindon between August 1945 and April 1947. By the end of 1963 all bar eight of the class had been withdrawn and, on 20 September 1964, the Stephenson Locomotive Society organised a farewell tour using No 1011 *County of Chester*, which was, by that date, the last of the type in service. The locomotive is seen here at speed taking the Didcot West curve heading towards Birmingham. The locomotive was to survive for a further two months; whilst none were preserved at the time, work is currently in hand on the construction of a 31st example. *Roy Hobbs/Online Transport Archive*

The ex-Cambrian Railways line from Dovey Junction towards Pwllheli runs along the coast for much of its route between the junction and Barmouth. On 26 September 1964 BR Standard 3 2-6-2T No 82006 heads northbound on the approaches to Aberdovey with a down service. *Roy Hobbs/Online Transport Archive*

MAIN IMAGE

It's the early morning of 27 November 1964 and Ivatt-designed 2-6-0 No 46521 heads westbound at Frankton Halt with a service from Whitchurch to Oswestry over the easternmost section of the former Cambrian Railways. By this date the line via Oswestry to Buttington Junction at Welshpool was approaching its closure; passenger services from Whitchurch to Welshpool were withdrawn on 18 January 1965 on which date the section from Ellesmere through Frankton Halt to Oswestry closed completely. *Roy Hobbs/Online Transport Archive*

TOP

On 28 November 1964 an unidentified Stanier-designed 'Jubilee' class 4-6-0 crosses the Cefn viaduct, south of Ruabon, with a Down service heading towards Chester and Birkenhead Woodside. The viaduct, completed in 1848, has 19 spans and extends for a length of 1,508ft with a maximum height above the ground of 147ft. It was designed by Henry Robinson with Thomas Brassey acting as contractor and is now Grade II* listed. *Roy Hobbs/Online Transport Archive*

MIDDLE

On 27 November 1964 BR Standard Class 3 2-6-2T No 82006 is seen again. It is pictured in green livery at Barmouth station awaiting the road. In all 45 of this class, a development by Riddles of the earlier GWR '61xx' class, were built at Swindon between April 1952 and August 1955 primarily for light passenger services primarily on the Western and Southern regions. A number, such as No 82006, were used on the Cambrian section. Following transfer, No 82006 was to end its career allocated to the Southern Region, being withdrawn from Stewarts Lane in September 1966. Although none of the class was preserved at the time, work is currently in progress in building a 46th example — No 82045 — on the Severn Valley Railway. *Roy Hobbs/Online Transport Archive*

BOTTOM

Following inter-regional transfers, the Western Region took over the ex-Southern line from Barnstaple Junction to Ilfracombe. On 27 March 1965 Collett-designed 0-6-0 No 3205 — which was subsequently to be preserved — is pictured passing through Wrafton station towards Ilfracombe. It then headed the 'Exmoor Ranger' railtour towards Taunton. Listed for closure in the Beeching report, the Ilfracombe branch closed on 5 October 1970; although there were plans for its preservation, these came to nothing. *Roy Hobbs/Online Transport Archive*

The last BR operated steam services were not those on the main line that ceased in August 1968 but those of the narrow gauge Vale of Rheidol line in Wales. The 1ft 11¾in gauge line from Aberystwyth to Devil's Bridge — a distance of almost 12 miles — was opened to passenger services on 22 December 1902. BR continued to operate the line through to its sale in 1989 and thus the locomotives were — as illustrated in this view of No 7 *Owain Glyndŵr* heading towards Devil' Bridge over the River Rheidol to the east of Llanbadarn during the summer of 1969 — the only steam locomotives to be painted in the 1964 blue livery with double-arrow logo. No 7 was, in 1989, to become the last locomotive to haul of BR timetabled steam service. *R. W. A. Jones/Online Transport Archive*

In 1923 the Great Western inherited a complex network of often competing lines in the Welsh Valleys that served, primarily, the local coal industry. Although there was some rationalisation of duplicate routes both before and after Nationalisation, even into the 1970s the coal industry continued to generate significant traffic for the surviving lines. The '56xx' class 0-6-2Ts were a post-Grouping design by Collett, based on an earlier class produced for the Rhymney Railway, built at Swindon between 1924 and 1928 to serve on coal trains in the Valleys. In all some 200 were produced with the first withdrawals not occurring until 1962. No 5681 — seen here at Bargoed between duties — was to survive until October 1965. *Roy Hobbs/Online Transport Archive*

One of the most spectacular viaducts constructed in South Wales was that situated near Taff Wells. Built by the Barry Railway, the seven-span Walnut Tree viaduct was completed in 1901. In later years, following the rationalisation of the route, the viaduct was retained solely to provide a headshunt for the dolomite quarry. During the 'Rambling 56 Railtour' of 31 July 1965, the special visited the remaining section and the train, headed by No 6643 is pictured on the headshunt. Following the line's final closure, the viaduct was demolished in 1969. *Roy Hobbs/Online Transport Archive*

Another section visited by the 'Rambling 56 Railtour' of 31 July 1965 was Bargoed where the train is pictured towards the end of the day. The Class 56xx 0-6-2T, of which 200 were constructed between 1924 and 1928, was designed by Collett for use in the valleys of South Wales for working coal trains. The 0-6-2T had been favoured by some of the smaller railways taken over by the GWR at Grouping in 1923 and the '56xx' was designed to replace some of the older locomotives that the GWR acquired in 1923. All had been withdrawn by the end of 1965. *Roy Hobbs/Online Transport Archive*